KS1 Success

Revision Guide

Lynn Huggins-Cooper

English

Contents

Reading

Reading and writing

Writing

Test practice

Answers and glossary

Alliteration

What is alliteration?

Alliteration is where a sound is **repeated lots of times** in a sentence or a piece of writing. The **author** uses it to create an effect.

If you were writing about a snake, for example, you might like to use lots of 'ssss' sounds, so that people reading your writing think about the noise a snake makes:

The sneaky snake slithered silently...

If you were writing about a fierce bear, you could make your readers think about roaring by repeating a 'rrrr' sound:

A ferocious bear rushed around, growling and roaring.

When you are looking for alliteration in a piece of writing, read it out loud so that you can hear the sounds.

Tongue-twisters

Do you know any **tongue-twisters**? They use lots of alliteration – that is what makes them hard to say! Try saying these tongue-twisting sentences to yourself. See how many times you can say them without making a mistake!

Try:

Around the rugged rocks the ragged rascal ran!
Big bad Betty bought bags and bags of broken biscuits.
Pretty Paula poked a prickly porcupine.

Funny poems

Funny poems often use alliteration (and rhyme) to make a funny effect. Read this short poem, then try to make up your own!

Freaky Frances
Likes wild dances.

Saucy Susie
is very choosy!

Mad Marion
will dance with anyone

But My Marie
will only dance with me!

Have a go...

Look at headlines in newspapers. They often use alliteration to make a funny headline. Make a collection of them, then try making up your own, to talk about events at home – Mum makes mountains of muffins!

Key words

author
tongue-twisters
alliteration

Quick Test

Which sound is repeated in each of these sentences?

1. Lovely Laura liked licking lollies.
2. Beautiful Betty bit a bagel.
3. Tricky tribes tried tracking troublesome Trevor.
4. Ghastly, gruesome ghosts grabbed Gordon!
5. Sophie says slugs are silly!

Syllables

What are syllables?

Syllables are **the different bits of sound you hear** in a word as you say it.

The word cat has one syllable

The word butterfly has three syllables: butt – er – fly

The word monkey has two syllables: mon – key

The word alligator has four syllables: all – i – gat – or

How many syllables are there in your name?

Counting syllables

A good way to count syllables is to **clap them as you say words.**

Try clapping these words and count the syllables.

Car

Motorbike

Bicycle

Helicopter

Aeroplane

Top Tip *Counting syllables by saying words out loud is easier than trying to count them in your head.*

Have a go...

Clap and count the syllables in your friends' names. Make the names into sets labelled one syllable, two syllables, etc. You could even make a graph on the computer to show which number of syllables is the most common!

Key words

syllables

Quick Test

Which word in each set has the most syllables?

1. donkey horse cow
2. poppy daffodil rose
3. puppy kitten elephant
4. spider ladybird slug
5. fish anemone seagull

Words that rhyme

What is a rhyme?

When we talk about words rhyming, we mean they contain the same sound or sound the same.

These words all **rhyme**:

bed and red
make and take
pet and vet
Cat and bat
Pin and bin
Pot and dot

Same sounds – different letters!

Words do not need to be spelt in the same way to rhyme. As long as the letters make the same sound, the words rhyme.

These words rhyme too!

head and bed
pie and cry
chair and bear
floor and more

Top Tip

Say words out loud and it is easy to tell if they rhyme or not. The letters 'ee', 'ea', 'ie' and 'y' can all make the same sound!

Poetry and rhyme

Poetry often, but not always, uses rhyme.

Read the poem below – it is a well-known nursery rhyme.

Humpty Dumpty sat on a wall,
Humpty Dumpty had a great fall!
All the King's horses and all the King's men
Couldn't put Humpty together again!

These words rhyme:

- Humpty and Dumpty
- wall and fall
- men and again

Have a go...

Can you think of any words that rhyme with your name?

Key words

rhyme

Quick Test

Find the word in each list that is the odd one out – because it does not rhyme with the others. Say them out loud so you can hear the sound each word makes.

1. cat bat fit fat
2. make cake late bake
3. trip pip stop dip
4. bun fun fan run
5. bit bat sit fit

Plurals – more than one

What does plural mean?

Plural is a way of describing **more than one**. When words are changed from meaning one thing (**singular**) to more than one thing (plural), there are special rules about the way the ending of the word changes.

With most words, we show that there is more than one by adding an -s to the end of the word:

cat ➔ cats   dog ➔ dogs   boy ➔ boys   girl ➔ girls   cake ➔ cakes

With words that already end in -s, we sometimes add -es:

bus ➔ buses   loss ➔ losses

Word endings

Some words have special rules when you change from one to more than one (plural).

With words that end in -o, you add -es for the plural.

potato ➔ potatoes   tomato ➔ tomatoes

With words that end in -y, you take away the -y, and add -ies for the plural.

lady ➔ ladies   pony ➔ ponies

With words that end in -f, you take away the -f, and add -ves for the plural.

leaf ➔ leaves   loaf ➔ loaves   calf ➔ calves   wife ➔ wives

Special words

There are some special words that change completely when you change from one to more than one (plural).

mouse ➔ mice   man ➔ men

Top Tip *You just have to learn these special words, like you learn spellings. Make some cards with the word for one (mouse) on one side and the plural (mice) on the other. Then test yourself!*

Have a go...

Play a game with a partner – perhaps an older brother or sister, or your parents. Take turns to say the word for one thing (leaf) that your partner has to change to a plural (leaves).

Key words

plural   singular

Quick Test

Change the words below to show that they have changed from one thing to plural (more than one):

1. Baby ➔
2. Lolly ➔
3. Bag ➔
4. Wolf ➔
5. Leaf ➔

Nouns and adjectives

What are nouns?

Nouns are the words used for **the names of people, places, animals and things.**

The cat ran into the garden.
'Cat' and 'garden' are the nouns in the sentence.

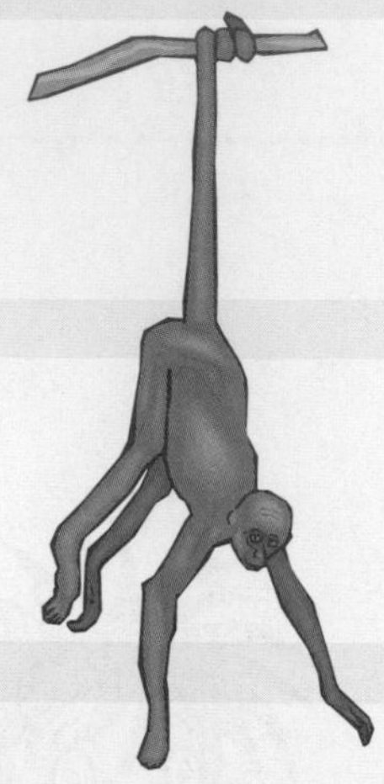

The monkey climbed the tree.
'Monkey' and 'tree' are the nouns in the sentence.

Bethany laughed at the joke.
'Bethany' and 'joke' are the nouns in the sentence.

I went to Brighton to play on the pier.
'Brighton' and 'pier' are the nouns in the sentence.

What are adjectives?

Adjectives are **describing words**. They describe a noun in a sentence.

The huge spider crawled into the dark corner.

'Huge' is the adjective that describes 'spider' and 'dark' is the adjective that describes 'corner'.

The sparkling star glittered in the velvet sky.

'Sparkling' is the adjective that describes 'star' and 'velvet' is the adjective that describes 'sky'.

The brown dog jumped over the wooden fence.

'Brown' is the adjective that describes 'dog' and 'wooden' is the adjective that describes 'fence'.

Top Tip

Sentences always have a noun – try and spot them when you are reading.

Have a go...

Look at a page in a storybook. Can you pick out all the nouns and all the adjectives?

Key words

nouns **adjectives**

Quick Test

Which words are nouns and which are adjectives in these sentences?

1. The fat mouse ate the smelly cheese.
2. The stripy bumblebee landed on the yellow flower.
3. The slimy slug ate the juicy leaf.
4. The pretty girl smiled.
5. The black dog barked very loudly!

Verbs and adverbs

What are verbs?

Verbs are the **words that describe actions.**

The girl is *playing*.

The word 'playing' is the verb.

The dog *barked*.

The word 'barked' is the verb.

The lion *roared*.

The word 'roared' is the verb.

The boy is *riding* his bike.

The word 'riding' is the verb.

Tense

Be careful to use the right **tense** of a verb. The tense of a verb tells you when something happened:

present – walk

past – walked

What are adverbs?

Adverbs are **words that describe verbs.**

The girl ran quickly.

The word 'quickly' is the adverb. It describes the verb 'ran', telling us how it was done.

The boy whispered quietly.

The word 'quietly' is the adverb. It describes the verb 'whispered', telling us how it was done.

The cat crept slowly into the barn.

The word 'slowly' is the adverb. It describes the verb 'crept', telling us how it was done.

Adverbs often (but not always) end in the letters 'ly'.

Have a go...

Play the 'adverb game'. Make a set of cards with verbs on – such as 'walk, talk, sing, play, swim', etc. Take a card, and the other players have to give you an adverb to describe the way you should act out your verb. Imagine – walking [verb] 'clumsily' [adverb] – it would be funny!

Key words

verbs
adverbs
tense

Quick Test

Which words are the verbs and adverbs in these sentences?

1. The rabbit jumped quickly.
2. The baby cried fiercely.
3. The boy ran quickly.
4. The man snored loudly.
5. The woman sang happily.

Learning your spellings

Look, cover, write, check

Have you tried this really easy way of learning new spellings? Follow these steps:

1 Look – Look at the shape of the word. Does it have any easy-to-remember shapes like a double 'oo' in the middle, like 'boot'? Or does it have any **tails** like the letters p or y? Perhaps it has **sticks** like d and b?

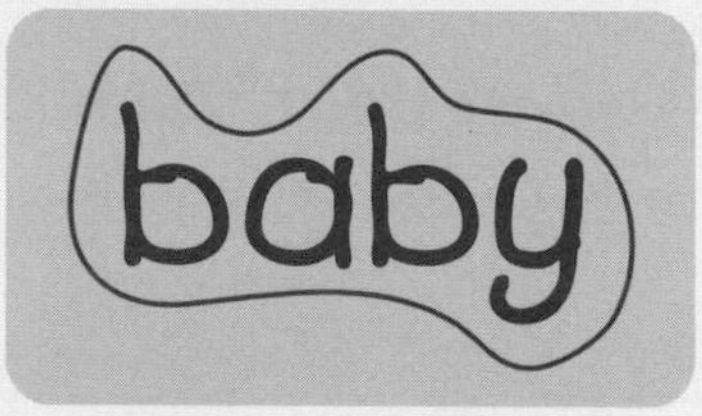

Baby has a stick at the beginning and a tail at the end.

2 Cover – Now cover the word you are trying to learn to spell.

3 Write – Try to write the word – see if you have a picture in your head of the shape of the word.

4 Check – Check the word. Is it right? If it is not, look again. Did you get some of the letters right? Have another go!

To help you to see the shape in your head, write the word you want to learn and draw a line around the outside of it, like a border. This will help you to remember the shape.

Spelling sounds

When you look at words that you are trying to spell, see if you can find the sounds in the words. This will help you, because lots of words use the same sounds. Be careful of **homophones** – words that sound the same but are spelt differently and mean different things – such as 'to', 'too' and 'two'.

For big, say 'b – ig'.

For pig, say 'p – ig'.

Just changing the first letter of 'big' to a 'p' changes it into a different word – 'pig'!

So if you learn that the sound 'ig' is spelt 'i – g', it will help you to spell lots of other words: big pig jig dig

For cat, say 'c – at'.

For bat, say 'b – at'.

Just changing the first letter of 'cat' to a 'b' changes it into a different word – 'bat'!

So if you learn that the sound 'at' is spelt 'a – t', it will help you to spell lots of other words: cat bat fat hat

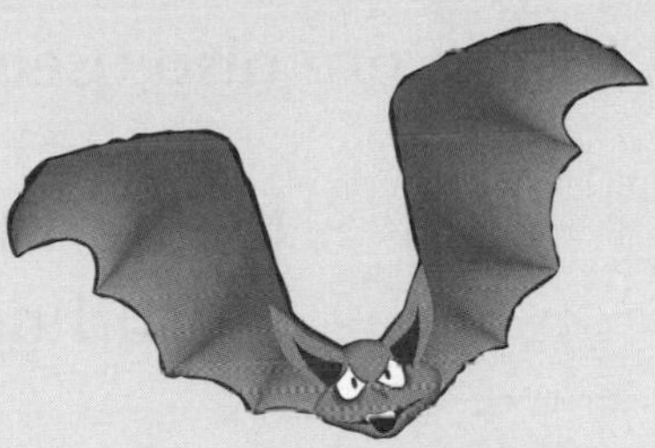

Have a go...

You can also look for words within words to help you to spell. 'Then' has 'hen' in the middle, just as 'will' has 'ill', 'that' has 'hat' and 'mend' has 'end' – at the end!

Can you think of any other words within words?

Key words

tails
homophones
sticks

Quick Test

How many words can you make by changing the first letter of these words?

1. Had (If you work your way through the alphabet from a to z, then the first word you will recognise will be bad, followed by dad, etc.)
2. Bin
3. Fall

Punctuation marks

Capital letters and lower case letters

Sentences always begin with a **capital letter**.

These are capital letters. They are also called **upper case letters**.

A B C D E F G H I J K L M N O P Q R S T U V W X Y Z

These are the same letters when they are not capitals. They are also called **lower case letters**.

a b c d e f g h i j k l m n o p q r s t u v w x y z

Capital letters are also used for **names of people and places**.

Sam Mel Mrs Nelson Mr Marsh London
Durham England Africa

Full stops

Full stops show that a sentence is finished. Most sentences – except questions and exclamations – end with a full stop.

I live on a farm**.** I have lots of animals including goats and rabbits**.** Yesterday, one of my horses had a foal**.** I need to think of a name for the baby horse**.**

? and !

These **punctuation marks** are very easy to use. If you ask a question, your sentence **does not end with a full stop** – it ends with a **question mark**. If you make an exclamation – like when you shout, or are excited – you use an **exclamation mark**.

Question marks:

- Do you like cheese on toast?
- What is your name?
- May I have a sweet?

Exclamation marks:

- That's terrible!
- How lovely!
- What a dreadful smell!

Top Tip

If you are writing and are not sure if a sentence should end in a question mark, read it out loud. If it sounds like a question, add a question mark!

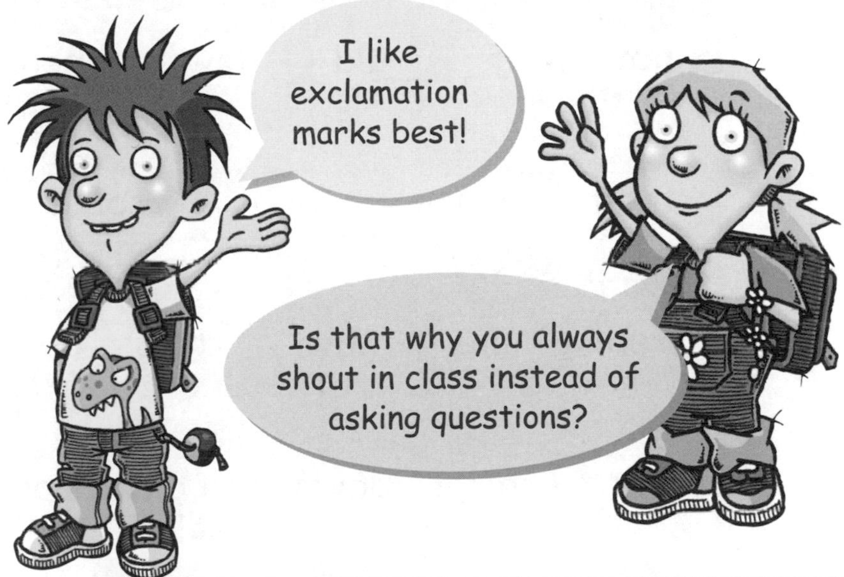

Have a go...

Are these questions or exclamations?

- *Do you want a drink*
- *I love cream cakes*
- *What's the time, please*
- *What a rude girl*

Key words

capital letter
upper case letters
lower case letters
full stops
punctuation marks
question mark
exclamation mark

Quick Test

Re-write these sentences using full stops and capital letters.

1. my name is rajan my favourite animals are cats
2. my name is sophie i come from london
3. my name is marie i come from durham i like music
4. my dog's name is moss
5. i like lions and tigers

Test your skills

The word snake game

What to do: Play this game to help you to learn to spell – and have fun at the same time!

1 Make a set of word cards by writing the following words in dark felt pen on pieces of paper or card cut from old packaging. These are common words that you will meet in the books you are reading.

he	we	it	so	with	he	and	an
him	the	old	big	we	at	been	my
not	if	did	how	where	but	her	end
then	make	right	could	would	will	kite	
went	me	have	can	our	only	over	with
that	she	down	look	because	into	they	
off	this	out	now	up	call	in	which
two	for	do	you	all	what	come	pop
get	or	one	here	was	be	pig	egg

2 Use card or paper and brightly coloured felt pens to make a snake's head. It should be quite big.

How to play

1 Lay a word card down so that one end is touching the snake's head. The example below uses the word 'two'.

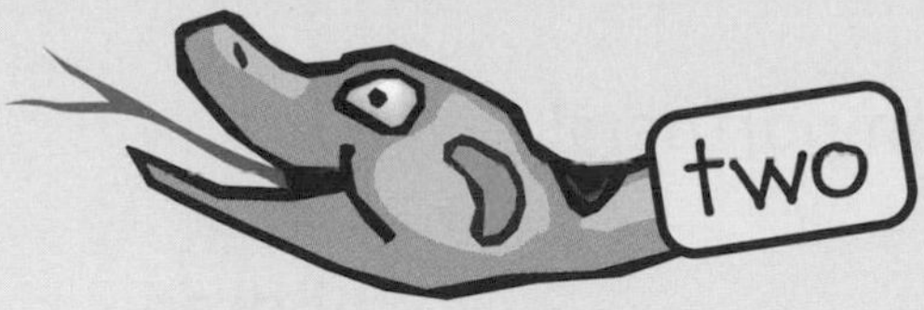

2 Then you have to find a word that starts with the last letter of the word before. In the example below, the word 'old' has been chosen.

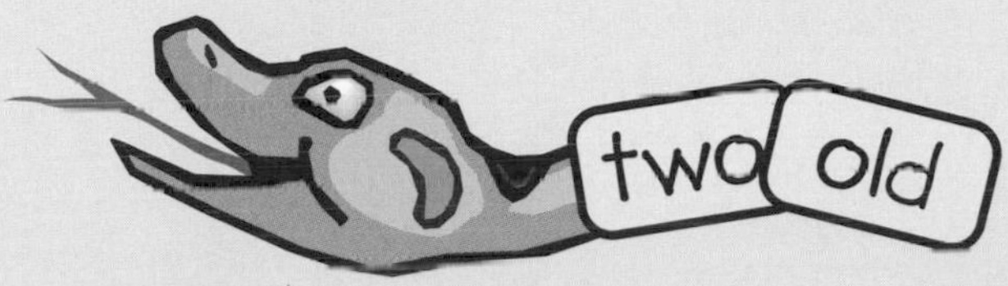

3 Carry on as long as you can, adding words each time that start with the last letter of the word before.

You can play this game in the car, by playing 'spelling I spy', thinking up the words instead of using cards. Play in the same way – starting the next word with the last letter of the previous word.

Test your knowledge

Section 1

1 Match the words to their alliteration partners!

slippery	children
bouncy	dungeon
chattering	balls
dark	slugs

2 How many syllables are there in each of these animals?

Alligator ______________ Horse ______________

Cat ______________ Rabbit ______________

Lion ______________ Tiger ______________

Antelope ______________

Section 2

3 Change these words from singular to plural:

Dog ______________ Mouse ______________

Lady ______________ Butterfly ______________

4 Which of these words rhyme with make?

cake paint take pipe bake land

____

____

Section 3

5 Which words in these sentences are nouns and which are adjectives?

a The tabby cat leapt in through the open window.

nouns ______________ adjectives ______________

b The huge slug slithered under the grey stone.

nouns ______________ adjectives ______________

c Ellie likes creamy toffees.

nouns ______________ adjectives ______________

d Canada is wonderful. There are lots of massive trees.

nouns ______________ adjectives ______________

Section 4

6 Which of the words in these sentences are verbs and which are adverbs?

a The fly buzzed noisily.

verb ______________ adverb ______________

b The horse galloped quickly.

verb ______________ adverb ______________

c The lady walked slowly.

verb ______________ adverb ______________

d The elephant marched heavily.

verb ______________

adverb ______________

Collecting story ideas

Collecting ideas

When writers are going to write a **story**, they usually have lots of ideas before they start. They often make **notes** to help them. One way to make notes is to do a map of your ideas on paper.

The ideas do not have to be written in full sentences. Look at this map of ideas for a story about a naughty goat:

Joining ideas

Once you have done a map of your ideas, you can put them into the order you want them to go in your story. You can join your ideas together with arrows to show how the story should be organised – you don't need to write all of your ideas out again!

Look at this **ideas map**. It doesn't look very tidy, but that doesn't matter. The map is to help you to organise your ideas.

Practice makes perfect!

Try making lots of story maps to get some practice. You can plan non-fiction, such as reports, in the same way.
You could also write a story map to plan an **article** for your school newsletter, if you have one.
Remember to tell your teacher about what you are doing!

Top Tip
Write down exciting words for your story as a part of your map. For a story about stars you could write: sparkly, glitter, fire, glow...

Have a go...

Here are some ideas for stories for you – you can write a story map for these titles – and then write the story!

- *The Haunted Castle*
- *The Garden of Secrets*
- *The Invisible Cat*
- *Caught in a Trap!*
- *A Horse of My Own*

Key words

story	ideas map
notes	article

Quick Test

Organise this story map by putting the ideas in the best order to tell the story.
The Magic Crystal

1. A girl finds a crystal
2. Crystal is glowing – pink then black
3. Girl sees evil dragon – and runs!
4. Girl runs into friendly troll, who helps her to escape
5. Girl spins through space into different world
6. Troll and girl find a cottage and live there happily forever

Writing a story plan

Making a plan

Story-planning sheets help you to organise your ideas for writing. If you practise planning at home, you will soon be an expert! There are certain things you need to think about whenever you are planning a story.

- What is your story about? You can't have a story without a subject!
- **Characters** in the story – all the action has to happen to someone (or something!).
- An **exciting beginning** – to excite the reader and make them want to read more.
- A **strong ending** – so your story doesn't just fizzle out.
- Lots of action!

The important questions

The important questions you must ask yourself are: **who, where, what, when and why!** To help you to plan, ask yourself the following questions:

1 WHO? Who is going to appear in your story? Are there goodies and baddies?

2 WHERE? Where is your story set? Remember to use lots of **description**! Don't just write 'in a house', but give us more detail so we can see it for ourselves, such as 'in a dark, spooky, old house'.

3 WHAT? What action is going to happen in your story?

4 WHEN? Set the scene – when does the action happen? Was it a long time ago or perhaps even in the future?

5 WHY? Give **reasons why things happen** in your story. Why do characters act the way they do?

How reading can help

When you read stories, make a note of ideas you really like. You could even keep a **notebook of ideas**. It is not copying – you are not going to write the same story. You are learning about how to write stories and the best way to learn is from other stories.

Top Tip

Read as many stories as you can – and think about the story when you watch a programme on television. You may get some ideas for writing your own stories!

Have a go...

Write your own story plan for one of these titles:

- *The Terrible Storm*
- *I Found a Mermaid!*
- *The Enormous Butterfly*
- *The Enchanted Mirror*

Key words

characters description

Quick Test

1. What are the five questions you should ask yourself when you are planning a story?
2. How can reading help you to write your own stories?
3. When you are practising your story-planning, what should you think about?
4. Why are story-planning sheets useful?
5. What is a *character*?

Exciting stories

Story starters

If a story has a really exciting beginning, **the reader will want to read more**. If it is boring, people will not want to read the rest of the story. Look at these two story starters.

It was dark. The girl walked down the garden path and saw the bushes rustling.

Crash! Ellie heard a noise from the darkness of the garden. She grabbed a torch and slowly walked down the path. Suddenly, the bushes started rustling!

Which story starter is more interesting? The second story starter is exciting because it has **more description**, which makes you want to find out what happens next.

Exciting endings

The way your story ends is very important. Try not to end with '... and they went home', or '... then they went home to bed'. Lots of people end their stories this way and you want to be different!

Try to make sure that your reader knows **what has happened to the characters in your story** at the end. Sometimes people forget to do this. A character pops up in a story and then disappears, because the writer forgets about them in the excitement of writing. That's why story plans are such a good idea (see page 26) – they help you to remember all the good ideas you have as you start to write.

Which one is your favourite?

Look at these two story endings. Which one do you prefer?

The noise in the dark garden was not a monster after all!

1 "I think someone reads too many spooky comics!" laughed Mum as she picked up the tiny hedgehog. The spiky creature had made the bushes rustle and had made the awful snuffling and snorting noises. "Come on, we'll find a warm box for this little fellow. He's too small to stay outside all winter. He can stay in my shed until spring."

2 Ellie smiled, feeling a bit embarrassed. She had been quite scared – and of a tiny hedgehog! Now she looked forward to helping her Mum to care for the little creature until he was big enough to set free, when the warm weather came.

The noise was not a monster. It was a hedgehog. Ellie's Mum put the hedgehog in a box in the shed. Then they all went to bed.

Which ending is more interesting? Without a doubt the first ending, because it has more action and explains what has happened.

Top Tip

Look at beginnings and endings of stories carefully. This will help you to get some good ideas for your own stories.

Have a go...

Re-read your favourite story. Have a go at writing a completely different ending!

Key words

paragraph

Quick Test

Write the first and last **paragraph** of a story about a mysterious stranger that visits your town. Make it exciting!

Speech marks

What are speech marks?

When you are writing and you want to show someone is speaking, you use **speech marks:** “ ”

“I like crisps,” said Mum.

Mum actually said the words, so they are put in speech marks.

Mum told me that she liked crisps.

Mum did not actually say the words, so they are not put in speech marks.

Remember – speech marks show that someone is actually speaking. If they are not actually speaking – you don’t need speech marks! Read the words out loud to help you to decide.

Different ways to say 'said'

Do not always use 'said', because it gets boring!

"Hello," said Beth.

"Hello," said Rai.

"Would you like a sweet?" said Beth.

"Yes, please," said Rai.

"Strawberry is my favourite," said Beth.

"My favourite is lime," said Rai.

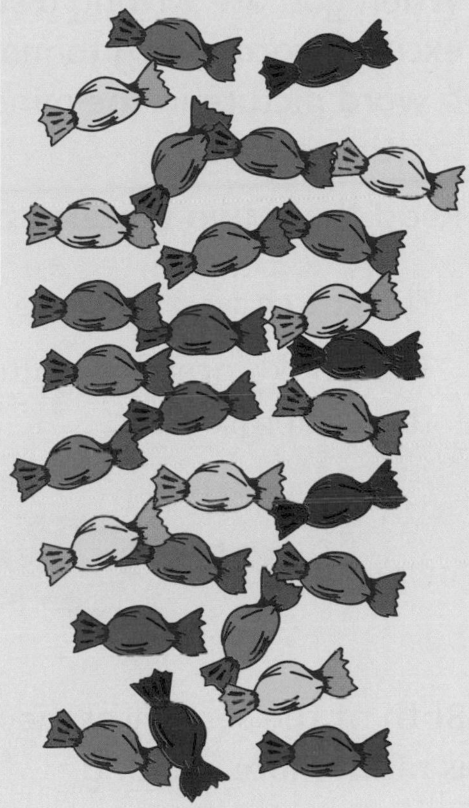

There are lots of other ways to say 'said'!
How many can you think of?

whispered	shouted
yelled	squealed
bellowed	asked

Have a go...

Look in books and comics and collect all the different words you can find for 'said'. Make a note of them – and use them when you write stories.

Key words

speech marks

Quick Test

Add the speech marks to these sentences:

1. I love rabbits! said Helen.
2. What's your name? asked Tina.
3. My favourite food is pizza, said John.
4. What's that awful smell? grumbled Jane.
5. I'd like a red lolly, please, said Betty.

Exciting descriptions

Great vocabulary

When you are writing a story, you need to use great descriptions and exciting **vocabulary** to make your story interesting. You can make a **word picture** in the mind of your readers, if your description is exciting enough!

Read these two sentences:

The cat chased a mouse into the bushes.

The smoky grey cat galloped after the fuzzy mouse, chasing it into the undergrowth.

Both of the sentences mean the same thing – but the second sentence is **much more exciting.**

Word pictures

When you are writing a story or a poem, think about the thing you are describing. **Try to see the thing in your head** – like a photograph. Then describe the thing as though you can see it and tell your reader what it looks like. Use your other senses, too – smell, touch, hearing and taste.

Read this description of strawberries.

I love ripe, juicy strawberries! They smell sweet, like candyfloss, and they shine like jewels. I love the way they squash in your mouth and all the juice explodes onto your tongue.

Could you picture them in your head?

Make a word collection!

When you are reading stories or comics – or when you are watching the television – listen for exciting, **descriptive** words. You could make a collection in a notebook. You may even like to choose words that are particulary enjoyable to say!

Start your collection with these:

slime fizz sparkle dazzle glow

Top Tip *Read lots of poetry – it often has wonderful descriptions and word pictures, and it will give you some ideas for your own work!*

Have a go...

Look at advertisements in magazines. They often have lovely descriptions to make you want to buy the thing they are advertising. Circle the descriptions you like best – or cut them out and make a collage.

Key words

vocabulary descriptive

Quick Test

Think of words to describe each of these things:

1. Spider
2. Rabbit
3. The sea
4. Snake
5. Shark

Similes and metaphors

What are similes?

A **simile** is a way of describing something by saying it is like something else. You will already use similes when you speak – and not realise it! Have you ever said:

It's as cold as ice in here!   My garden's like a jungle!

Similes make writing more interesting. They help to make word pictures in the reader's head. Read these examples:

The sand was **like brown sugar**, running through my hands.

The newt was **like a bulgy-eyed alien**, swimming around the pond.

The teacher stood there **like a volcano**, waiting to erupt.

Similes often describe something as like something else – so look out for the word 'like' to give you a clue. The word 'as' can also be a clue to finding similes: 'My hand was as cold as ice.'

What is a metaphor?

A **metaphor** is a way of describing something by saying it actually is something else. It does not mean that the thing you are describing really changes into something else, though!

Metaphors make **very strong word pictures** in the reader's head. Read these examples:

The pebble **was a sparkling jewel**, on the beach.

The cat **was a panther**, stalking through the grass.

The sun **was an orange**, glowing in the sky.

Which is it?

So how do I know if a description is a simile or a metaphor?

Similes and metaphors do the same thing, so it can be confusing. Try to remember that similes say **something *is like* something else** and metaphors say that **something *is* something else.**

'The rain *was like* a waterfall' is a simile, but 'The rain *was* a waterfall' is a metaphor.

'The sea *was like* an angry dog, charging up the beach' is a simile, but 'The sea *was* an angry dog, charging up the beach' is a metaphor.

'The wind *was like* a lonely ghost, moaning through the windows' is a simile, but 'The wind *was* a lonely ghost, moaning through the windows' is a metaphor.

Have a go...

When you are reading poems, see if you can find any descriptions that are similes or metaphors. Can you tell the difference?

Key words

simile **metaphor**

Quick Test

Which of these descriptions are similes and which are metaphors?

1. The flower was a fairy, dancing in the breeze.
2. The snow was like icing sugar, dusting a cake.
3. The slug was like a rubber toy, sliding across the path.
4. The fly was a fighter plane, dive-bombing my head.
5. The worm was like a snake, coiling on the ground.

Test your skills

Write a story

You are going to plan and write a story about a boy and girl on holiday at the seaside, who discover strange goings-on in a spooky old cave...

Map your ideas

Walk – find cave

Boy and girl on holiday – they would rather have gone somewhere hot and are bored.

Strange noises, dark – ghosts?

Story plan

Get your ideas in order!

Who? ➔ What? ➔ Where? ➔ When? ➔ Why?

The beginning...

Have you thought of a really exciting beginning? What about:

"But I want to go to Florida, not Boring-by-Sea!" shouted Sophie.

OR:

The children peered into the mouth of the cave. Strange, twisted rocks looked like people in the darkness.

...the end

Have you thought of a good ending? What about:

"I think that's as much excitement as anybody needs!" said Luke. The sea glittered and the children walked away along the cliffs.

Descriptions

Have you included some great descriptions, such as similes and metaphors? What about:

The sunlight sparkled on the water like broken glass.

The gulls circled, crying like lost children.

The cave was a huge, gaping mouth, ready to eat them up!

Your turn

Now write your story!

Test your knowledge

Section 1

Circle the descriptive words in each sentence.

1 The snail bumbled across the leaf, leaving a trail of sticky slime.

2 The moths danced in the moonlight, fluttering like petals in the darkness.

3 The toad sat on the log like a warty old witch.

4 The cat's eyes glittered like fire.

5 The branches of the tree scratched the window like a monster, waiting to get in.

6 The boy was so excited, he fizzed like a firework.

7 The dog twitched in his sleep, dream-rabbits making his throat rumble like far-away thunder.

8 The swallow twirled around my head, cutting the air with her sharp wings.

Section 2

Can you put the speech marks in the right place?

1 I love chocolate, said Helen.

2 Would you like a glass of orange? asked Mr Stirling.

3 Can I help you? asked the shop assistant.

4 That's mine! shouted Judith.

5 Let's go to the beach, said Lindsay.

6 I'd like a double lolly choc-bomb, please, giggled Sunita.

Section 3

Write down whether each sentence is a simile or a metaphor.

1 The bat whirled around the cloud of moths like a pilot in a black fighter plane. ____________________

2 The guinea pig was an eating machine, chomping through the apple. ____________________

3 The foal's legs were as delicate as fine bone china. ____________________

4 The spider lurked under the bed, a tiny furry monster hiding in the darkness. ____________________

5 The butterfly flexed her wings, like a girl trying on a beautiful new dress. ____________________

Writing letters

Informal language

Everyone likes getting letters! When the postman brings something for you, it is very exciting. Letters from friends are full of chatty news, but letters from school, for instance, use very different language.

Letters to friends and family use something called **informal language**. That just means chatty words, written like you speak them. Postcards and notes to friends are also written using informal language.

Informal language often uses **contractions**. A contraction is where two words are shortened to one and an **apostrophe** is used to show where a letter or some letters are missing.

is not → isn't   does not → doesn't   I am → I'm

An informal letter to a friend

This letter is written to a friend, so it uses informal language. See if you can find examples.

Hi Daisy!

I've just got back from my holidays and guess what? Sprite has had her foal! It's so tiny and fragile, you'd think its legs couldn't hold it up! You'll have to come really soon to see it.

Aargh! Back to school next week. We'll be in old Clarkie's class this year. Still – could've been worse, eh?

Talk to you later!

Love,

Midge.

You can tell this is an informal letter because:

- It starts with 'Hi!'
- There are lots of exclamation marks, because the **writer is excited**.
- Words are often used in their shortened versions: I've, it's, you'll, etc.
- It ends with 'Love'.
- The writer signs using her nickname.

Top Tip

Remember, when you write to friends and close relatives, you can write words exactly as you would say them.

Have a go...

Look at postcards and letters from friends to see what informal language looks like. Compare them with ***formal*** *letters – like letters from school – and see if you can spot differences in the language used.*

Key words

informal language
contraction
apostrophe
formal

Quick Test

Turn these shortened, informal versions of words into the formal version.

Example: Couldn't → could not

1. Don't →
2. Won't →
3. It's →
4. Can't →
5. Didn't →

Writing non-fiction

What is non-fiction?

Non-fiction is writing that is about real things – not things which are imagined or made up. If you wrote an article about your pet for the school paper, for instance, it would be non-fiction. Recipes are also non-fiction, and so are **instructions** telling people how to do things.

Non-fiction needs to be planned in a similar way to stories. You need to think about using interesting language and how you will organise your work. Instructions would be useless if they were not in the right order – and so would recipes!

Writing instructions

When you write instructions, **you need to think through, step-by-step**, what you have to do. **Make notes first** to make sure you get things in the **right order**.

Read these instructions for making a bat-flapper.

1 Fold a piece of paper in half.
2 Draw half a bat shape, starting with the body, on the fold.
3 Cut out the shape.
4 Colour the bat with paints or pens. White correction fluid makes good fangs!
5 Cut a piece of thread and stick one end to the bat's head.
6 Stick the other end to a straw or stick.
7 Wave the stick around to watch your bat flap!

If the instructions had been in the wrong order, you would not have found it easy to make a bat-flapper!

Writing a report

Read the following ideas for a **report** on a school visit to a lighthouse. When planning a report, write down everything that comes into your head. You don't have to use all of your first ideas, but thinking freely in this way will spark your imagination.

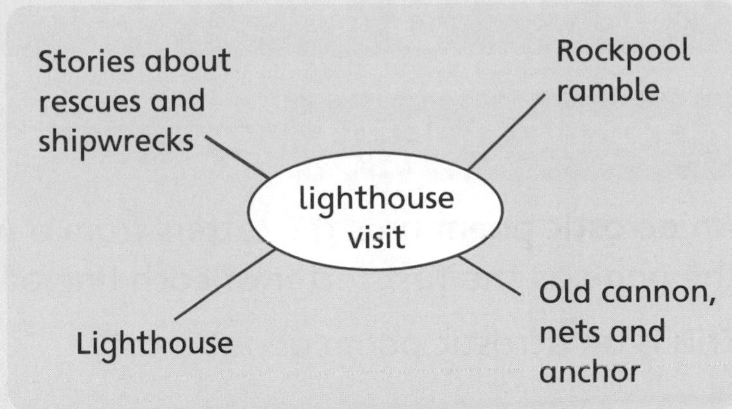

Now read the report.

Yesterday, we went to St. Mary's Island at Whitley Bay. We climbed the 137 steps to the top of the lighthouse. Downstairs, we looked at displays about wildlife around the island. My favourite bit was the 'pretend rockpool' that showed a close-up view of crabs, fish and anemones.

After lunch, we went outside. The garden had special plants that could live by the sea. There was a brilliant cannon and a huge black anchor. We went on a 'rockpool ramble'. We saw hermit crabs peeping out of shells. I liked the blenny (a fish), because it had big rubbery lips like a clown. We heard some scary stories about shipwrecks. I can't wait to go again!

Top Tip

Shine some light on your idea! Write your title in a circle. Then write your notes and ideas on lines coming out of the circle to make a sun shape.

Have a go...

Write a plan for a report on a school visit, a trip out with your family, or describing your favourite game. Then write the report!

Key words

non-fiction
report
instructions
fiction

Quick Test

1. How is non-fiction different from **fiction**?
2. Is a recipe fiction or non-fiction?
3. Do you need to write a plan when you write non-fiction?
4. Why is the order of instructions important?
5. Why is it a good idea to make notes of your ideas?

Writing poems

Acrostic poems

An **acrostic poem** uses the letters from a word written down the side of the page as the first letter of each line of the poem.

This is an acrostic poem about a cat.

Cuddly and soft
Always there for me to stroke
Tiny tiger on my bed.

The letters C A T are used as the first letter of each line. The poem explores the poet's ideas about her cat.

Shape poems

Shape poems are written in the shape of the thing they describe.

This is a shape poem about a monster.

My monster is fierce and dark.
When he roars
His furry jaws open wide.
Watch out!
He might eat you...
But he prefers jam sandwiches!

Top Tip

Have a look at this great website about poetry for children: http://www.childrenspoetrybookshelf.co.uk

Have a go...

*Write an acrostic poem using your name. Write your name down the side of your page, and make sure each line starts with a letter from your name. The poem should describe the **poet** – you!*

Key words

acrostic poem **poet**
shape poems

Quick Test

Write your own shape poem. Choose something you find interesting, such as an animal, a vehicle or a planet. Write a rough draft of your poem, then when you are ready, draw a shape and write your poem on it.

Reading comprehension

What is comprehension?

Comprehension means understanding. When you do comprehension exercises, it means you **answer questions to show that you understand** what you have read.

When you do a reading comprehension exercise, you should read through the passage once, to make sure you understand it. Then read the questions and look for the answers in the passage. This sounds really hard, but you can make it quite simple by learning a few tricks.

- **Skimming**
- Looking for **key words**

If you don't understand a question in a comprehension test, leave it and answer the others first. By the time you go back to it, you might have found out the answer!

Skimming and key words

What is skimming and what are key words?

When you are doing a reading comprehension, first you will read the passage through, then you will read the questions. After you have done this, look back at the passage again, skimming through – in other words, **reading quickly**. This will help you to find the **right part of the passage to answer your question**.

If you look at each question, you should be able to find important or key words.

In the question 'What sort of animal lives in a sett?' the key words are animal and sett, so you would look for these words in the passage:

'If you are very lucky and can sit quietly, you may see that most playful, yet fierce of creatures, the badger. Badgers live in their homes, called setts, deep in the woods.'

Once you found the key words 'sett' and the name of the animal, you would know you had found the answer to the question: badgers live in setts.

Have a go...

*Read a **double page spread** in a non-fiction book and write some questions. Can your friend find the answers? (Make sure you know them!)*

Key words

comprehension
skimming
key words
double page spread

Quick Test

1. What does 'comprehension' mean?
2. What does a comprehensive test do?
3. What are key words?
4. What is skimming?
5. Why should you read a passage through once before you try to answer the questions?

Test your skills

Reading comprehension

Read about Sprite's foal, then answer the questions.

Sprite is three years old. She lives in a field with her mother, Khola. Sprite and her mother are Welsh Cobs, a special breed of horse. Khola is a coloured horse, which means she is white with black and brown patches. She looks just like the horses in old cowboy films on the television! Sprite is white all over, except for a black splash on her face.

Yesterday, Sprite had a baby of her own. He doesn't have a name yet. Sprite's baby looks just like his Grandma! A baby horse is called a foal. The foal feeds on its mother's milk at first, then on grass, hay and horse feed.

Questions

1 What sort of animal is Sprite? Sprite is a horse

2 How old is she? She is three

3 What is Sprite's mother called? Khola

4 What markings does a coloured horse have? wite with blak brown patches

5 What is the name of the special breed of horses that Khola, Sprite and the foal belong to? Welsh cobs

6 What colour is Sprite? Wite with blak splash

7 What is a baby horse called? He doesnt have a name

8 What does a foal eat? grass hay and horse

Top Tip

Remember:

- *Read the whole passage.*
- *Read the questions.*
- *Skim through the passage looking for the answers.*
- *Read the passage through again.*
- *Check your answers.*

Answers

Did you enjoy reading about Khola and Sprite? See how many of the answers you got right:

1 A horse.

2 She is three.

3 She is called Khola.

4 White with black and brown patches.

5 They belong to the Welsh Cob breed.

6 White all over, except for a black splash on her face.

7 A foal.

8 Its mother's milk at first, then grass, hay and horse feed.

Test your knowledge

Section 1

Write a letter to your friend, telling them about your trip to the zoo. You can make this letter up, about an imaginary trip if you prefer.

Remember:

- Use informal language
- Use interesting descriptions
- Finish your letter with 'Love' or 'Love from'

Ideas to include:

- Your favourite animal
- Did you see any animals being fed?
- What did you have for lunch?
- Did you buy anything at the shop?

Section 2

Write a letter from your mum or dad to your teacher, explaining that you would like to take packed lunches to school instead of having school dinners.

Remember:

- Use formal language
- Finish your letter with 'Yours sincerely' rather than 'Love' or 'Love from'

Ideas to include:

- Why you would prefer a packed lunch
- Ask where people eat packed lunches
- Ask if there are any particular things you are not supposed to take. For instance, are you allowed to take cans?

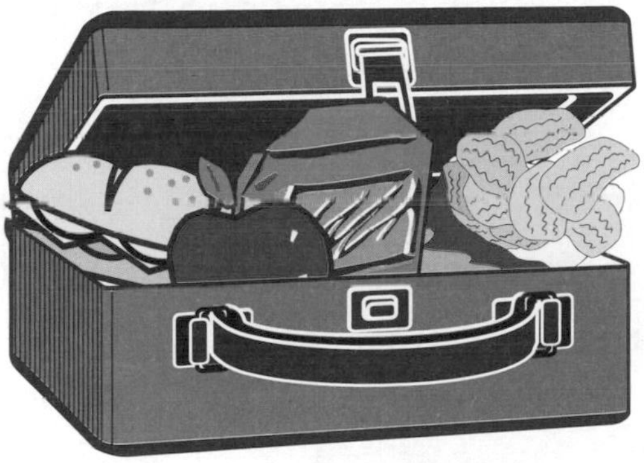

Test practice

Story task

1 Read the story starter below, then use it to help you write a story. The story is about a girl from another planet who is marooned on Earth.

> Story Starter
>
> The sky was filled with lights, as though showers of stars were falling to Earth. Isobel watched from her bedroom window as the coloured flames lit up the night. Suddenly, down in the garden, she saw something moving. As she looked closer, she realised it was a little girl!

Fill in the brainstorm to help you organise your ideas. Some words have been added to help you get started.

sparkling yellow eyes

clever

With beautiful brown hair

and she was a Pritty girl in a pinck dress

magic

scared of cats

Writing a plan

2 Now write a story plan – remember to ask yourself:

The important questions – who, where, what, when and why!

To help you to plan, ask yourself the following questions:

Who? Who is going to appear in your story? Are there goodies and baddies?

Where? Where is your story set? Remember to use lots of descriptions! Not 'in a wood', but 'in a wild, spooky wood'!

What? What action is going to happen in your story?

When? Set the scene – when does the action happen? Was it a long time ago, or even in the future?

Why? Give reasons why things happen in your story. Why do characters act in the way they do?

Remember – you can collect ideas and special words from books you read to help you to write your story!

Writing non-fiction

1 Writing Instructions

Think of something you have made, either at home or at school. It could be a model, a game, a piece of artwork – whatever you like! Write clear instructions so that someone else can follow them. It is very important that you put the instructions in the right order, so think carefully!

Remember to include:

- What you need
- What to do

2 Writing a Letter

Write to a friend, telling them about your pets or a pet you would like to have. Remember to use lots of descriptions to make your letter interesting!

You could include:

- What your pet looks like
- Funny things they do
- What you have to do to look after your pet

3 Make a Book

Choose one of the topics in the list or write about your hobby. Plan out what you will include, then look for pictures from magazines to help to illustrate your book. Make the book from pieces of paper stapled or stitched together – ask an adult to help you.

- Animals
- Dragons and dinosaurs
- Machines
- Space
- Insects
- Parties

4 Write a Book Review

Think of a book you have read and enjoyed and write about it. Try to make other people want to read the book too!

Remember to write about:

- The characters
- The action
- Are there illustrations?
- Was it a good ending?

Top Tip *Look in comics for pages that tell you how to make things. This will help you to write instructions.*

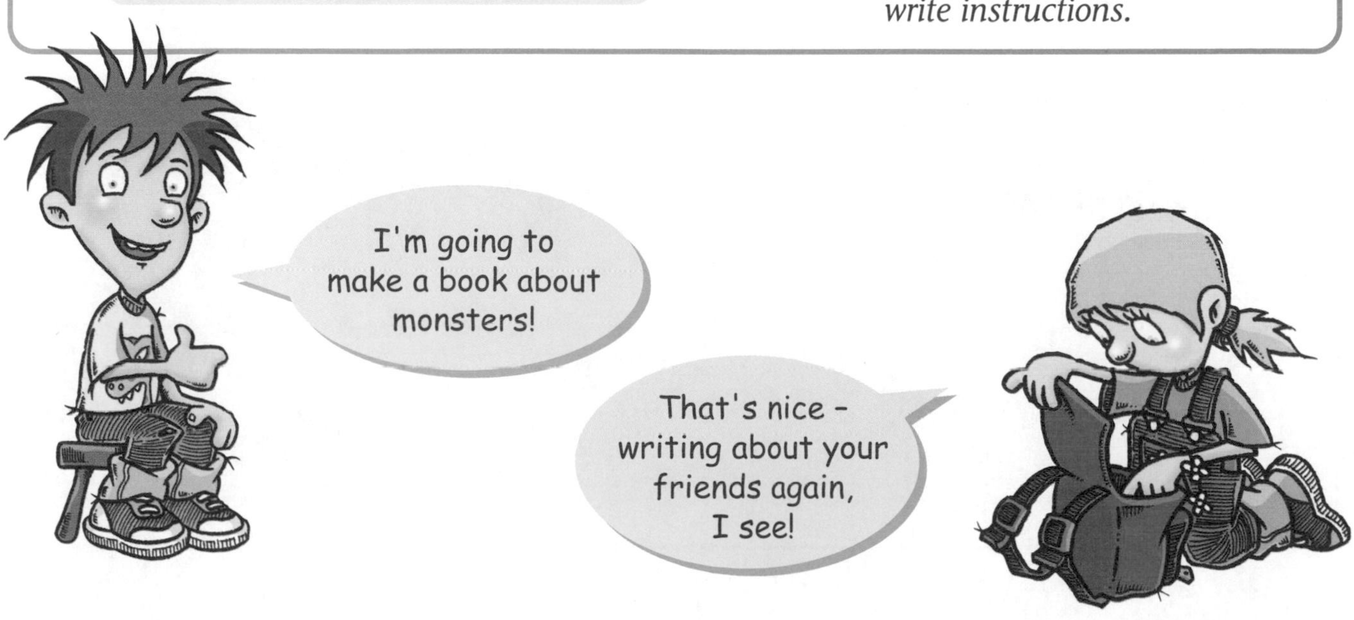

Comprehension

Read the story about Grendal, the farm cat, then answer the questions. Your answers will help to show if you have understood the story.

Grendal lay on the warm stone wall, soaking up the sun. He loved to sit there, watching in the grass for the tiny mice, who lived in the wall. His tail twitched lazily, like a big furry caterpillar. He watched the beautiful peacock butterflies as they sat on the daisies in the garden.

Nearby, Gracie and Sweetpea, the goats, were eating grass. They munched happily in the warm sun.

Suddenly, the goats popped their heads up from their meal, listening to a familiar noise – it was the farmer's car as it drove slowly up the bumpy lane. The goats began to bleat, making excited little noises as they thought about the food the farmer would bring. They loved it when there were slices of old bread in the feed bag.

Grendal heard the car, too. He looked up, then started to stalk up the lane, through the hedge, as though he was hunting. As the farmer slowed down, her car window was open. She saw the goats and stopped the car. She was bending across to pick up a bag of stale bread for Gracie and Sweetpea when she suddenly screamed – sharp claws had dug into her back!

She jumped out of the car, hopping up and down. What had poked her? Then she saw him. Grendal was in the car, with his front paws on the dashboard as he looked out of the front window. He looked just like one of the farmer's dogs, waiting to be taken on a trip out. He had leapt in through the window, using her as a stepping stone!

"Grendal, you are the funniest cat in the world!" laughed the farmer.

Questions

1 What sort of animal is Grendal?

farm cat

2 Where does he like to sit when it is warm?

warm stone wall

3 What animals does Grendal look for in the grass?

in the grass the tiny mice

4 Who are Gracie and Sweetpea?

goat

5 Why do the goats look up when they are eating the grass?

Because the goats heard farmer's car and thought farmer will bring them food!

6 Why does the farmer scream?

She felt sharp claws had dug into her back.

7 How had Grendal managed to get into the car?

Grendal had leapt in through the window using the farmer as a stepping stone.

8 How do you know that the farmer thinks Grendal is funny?

Top Tip

Remember to read the whole passage through once before you try to answer the questions. Then read the questions very carefully, so that you do not make silly mistakes.

Spelling test

You will need a grown-up to help you with this test. Ask them to read the passage to you. Then you should try to spell the words (writing them down) that they ask you to. If there are any spellings you find hard, look at pages 16–17 to help you to learn them.

Note to grown-ups – the words that need to be written down are underlined. Read the passage through to your child once, then a second time, pausing after each spelling to let them write the word.

Ellie ran down the bank to the edge of the pond. When she reached the stones, she stopped to take off her shoes. Paddling in the cool water, she saw what looked like a tiny dragon peering at her from under a rock. She moved closer to have a look. What could it be? She must find out! Walking slowly, so that she did not scare the creature away, she picked up her plastic bucket from the stones. With a splash, she caught the tiny creature and put it carefully into her nature box.

"Mum – look! A baby dragon!" she called. Her mum came across and peered into the box.

"It's a newt, Ellie. It does look like a dragon, doesn't it! He's lovely. You can tell it's a boy from the lovely orange crest on his back. Put it back carefully now, won't you?"

Answers

Reading

PAGES 4–5 ALLITERATION

1 l 2 b 3 tr 4 g 5 s

PAGES 6–7 SYLLABLES

1 donkey
2 daffodil
3 elephant
4 ladybird
5 anemone

PAGES 8–9 WORDS THAT RHYME

1 fit
2 late
3 stop
4 fan
5 bat

PAGES 10–11 PLURALS – MORE THAN ONE

1 Babies
2 Lollies
3 Bags
4 Wolves
5 Leaves

PAGES 12–13 NOUNS AND ADJECTIVES

noun = n adjective = adj

1 mouse, cheese (n) fat, smelly (adj)
2 bumblebee, flower (n) stripy, yellow (adj)
3 slug, leaf (n) slimy, juicy (adj)
4 girl (n) pretty (adj)
5 dog (n) black (adj)

PAGES 14–15 VERBS AND ADVERBS

verb = v adverb = adj

1 jumped (v), quickly (adv)
2 cried (v), fiercely (adv)
3 ran (v), quickly (adv)
4 snored (v), loudly (adv)
5 sang (v), happily (adv)

PAGES 16–17 LEARNING YOUR SPELLINGS

any words that rhyme

PAGES 18–19 PUNCTUATION MARKS

1 **M**y name is Rajan. **M**y favourite animals are cats.
2 **M**y name is Sophie. **I** come from London.
3 **M**y name is Marie. **I** come from Durham. **I** like music.
4 **M**y dog's name is **M**oss.
5 **I** like lions and tigers.

PAGES 22–23 TEST YOUR KNOWLEDGE

Section 1

1 slippery slugs / bouncy balls / chattering children / dark dungeon

2 Alligator : 4 Horse : 1
Cat : 1 Rabbit : 2
Lion : 2 Tiger : 2
Antelope : 3

Section 2

3 Dog : Dogs Mouse : Mice
Lady : Ladies Butterfly : Butterflies

4 cake, take, bake

Section 3

5 adjective = adj noun = n

a The **tabby** (adj) **cat** (n) leapt in through the **open** (adj) **window** (n).
b The **huge** (adj) **slug** (n) slithered under the **grey** (adj) **stone** (n).
c **Ellie** (n) likes **creamy** (adj) toffees (n).
d **Canada** (n) is **wonderful** (adj). There are lots of **massive** (adj) **trees** (n).

Section 4

6 verb = v adverb = adv

a The fly **buzzed** (v) **noisily** (adv).
b The horse **galloped** (v) **quickly** (adv).
c The lady **walked** (v) **slowly** (adv).
d The elephant **marched** (v) **heavily** (adv).

Reading and writing

PAGES 24–25 COLLECTING STORY IDEAS

The best order would be: 1, 2, 5, 3, 4, 6

PAGES 26–27 WRITING A STORY PLAN

1 who, where, what, when, why
2 It will give you ideas.
3 exciting beginning, characters, what happens, description, strong ending
4 They help you to think about your ideas and get them organised.
5 Characters are the people in your story.

PAGES 28–29 EXCITING STORIES

any first and last paragraph of a story about a stranger, with clear attempts to make it exciting

PAGES 30–31 SPEECH MARKS

1 "I love rabbits!" said Helen.
2 "What's your name?" asked Tina.
3 "My favourite food is pizza," said John.
4 "What's that awful smell?" grumbled Jane.
5 "I'd like a red lolly, please," said Betty.

PAGES 32–33 EXCITING DESCRIPTIONS

any interesting descriptions

PAGES 34–35 SIMILES AND METAPHORS

m = metaphor   s = simile

1 m **2** s **3** s **4** m **5** s

PAGES 38–39 TEST YOUR KNOWLEDGE

Section 1

1 The snail **bumbled** across the leaf, leaving a trail of **sticky slime**.
2 The moths **danced in the moonlight, fluttering like petals** in the darkness.
3 The toad sat on the log like **a warty old witch**.
4 The cat's eyes **glittered like fire**.
5 The branches of the tree scratched the window **like a monster, waiting to get in**.
6 The boy was so excited, he **fizzed like a firework**.
7 The dog twitched in his sleep, dream-rabbits making his throat **rumble like far-away thunder**.
8 The swallow twirled around my head, **cutting the air with her sharp wings**.

Section 2

1 "I love chocolate," said Helen.
2 "Would you like a glass of orange?" asked Mr Stirling.
3 "Can I help you?" asked the shop assistant.
4 "That's mine!" shouted Judith.
5 "Let's go to the beach," said Lindsay.
6 "I'd like a double lolly choc-bomb, please," giggled Sunita.

Section 3

m = metaphor   s = simile

1 s **2** m **3** s **4** m **5** s

Writing

PAGES 40–41 WRITING LETTERS

1 Do not
2 Will not
3 It is
4 Cannot
5 Did not

PAGES 42–43 WRITING NON-FICTION

1 It is about real things – and is not made up or imagined.
2 non-fiction
3 Yes, to help you to organise your ideas.
4 If they are out of order it would be hard to use instructions to make things, etc.
5 to help you to remember everything you want to include.

PAGES 44–45 WRITING POEMS

any poem, written on the appropriate shape

PAGES 46–47 READING COMPREHENSION

1 understanding
2 it tests that you have understood what you have read
3 important words that help you to find the right part of a passage to answer a question
4 a quick re-read to find the key words that will help you to answer the questions
5 it helps you to understood what it is about, and makes answering the questions much easier

PAGES 50–51 TEST YOUR KNOWLEDGE

Section 1

Any letter to a friend is fine. Don't worry too much at this stage about spelling or handwriting, but concentrate on what your letter is about.

Remember:

- Use informal language: you can use isn't, wasn't, can't, etc.
- Use interesting descriptions: make word pictures in your friend's head so he or she can see what you are talking about.
- Finish your letter with 'Love' or 'Love from'.

Did you include these ideas?

- Your favourite animal
- Did you see any animals being fed?
- What did you have for lunch?
- Did you buy anything at the shop?

Section 2

Any letter to school is fine. Don't worry too much at this stage about spelling or handwriting, but concentrate on what your letter is about.

Remember:

- Use formal language: not shortened words such as don't or can't.
- Finish your letter with 'Yours sincerely' rather than 'Love' or 'Love from'.

Did you include:

- Why you would prefer a packed lunch?
- A question about where people eat packed lunches?
- A question about any particular things you are not supposed to take, for example, cans?

Test practice

PAGES 52–58 TEST PRACTICE

Story task

child's own words for developing the story

Writing a plan

child's own story planned in idea/note form

Writing non-fiction

1 child's list of instructions including, what you need and what to do
2 child's letter about their pet including, what the pet looks like, funny things they do and what the child has to do to look after the pet
3 child's hand made book, many subjects possible
4 child's book review made interesting, taking into consideration the characters, the action, are there illustrations and was it a good ending

Comprehension

1 Grendal is a cat.
2 Grendal likes to sit on the stone wall when it is warm.
3 Grendal looks for mice in the grass.
4 Gracie and Sweetpea are goats.
5 The goats look up because they hear the farmer's car coming.
6 The farmer screams because something pokes her hard in the back.
7 Grendal had jumped into the car through the open window.
8 We know that the farmer thinks Grendal is funny because she laughs and says, "Grendal, you are the funniest cat in the world!"

Spelling test

all words spelt correcty

Glossary

acrostic poem a poem which uses a letter from a given word at the beginning of each line

adjective a describing word that describes a noun, e.g. the huge (adjective) cat (noun) growled

adverb describes a verb and tells us how it was done – for example, quietly, softly, quickly

alliteration repeating sounds in a sentence, e.g. the slimy slug slithered

apostrophe a punctuation mark sometimes used to show letters have been missed out

article a piece of writing, like those found in a newspaper or magazine

author a writer – someone who writes stories or non-fiction

capital letters upper case letters – used at the beginning of a sentence and for names of places and people

characters people in a story

comprehension a test of how much you have understood of a piece of writing

contraction where two words are shortened to one and an apostrophe is used to show where a letter or some letters are missing, e.g. I am → I'm

description writing about what something is like

descriptive writing that describes something well

double page spread two pages in a book or magazine that are opposite each other

exclamation mark a punctuation mark that is used to show an exclamation or someone shouting, such as 'Help!'

fiction made-up writing – such as stories

formal (language) language which is very 'correct', having no shortened words, slang, etc. Formal language is used in official letters

full stop a punctuation mark used at the end of a sentence, unless a question mark or exclamation mark has been used instead

homophones words that sound the same, but are spelt differently and mean different things, like 'to', 'too' and 'two'

ideas map helps you to organise your ideas, ready for writing a story or report

informal language language which is casual, using shortened words, slang, etc. Informal language is used in letters to friends

instructions a piece of writing that tells you how to do something

key words the most important words in a piece of writing – they tell you what it is all about

lower case letters small letters – not capitals. abcde… are lower case letters

metaphor a way of describing something by saying it is something else, e.g. 'The sun was a lantern, hanging in the sky.'

non-fiction reports, recipes, instructions – any writing that is not imaginary or made-up

notes ideas jotted down on paper

noun a naming word – the name for a thing, person or place

paragraph a separate section in a piece of writing made up of one or more sentences

plural describes more than one

poet a person who writes poetry

punctuation marks all the following are different types of punctuation: full stops, commas, exclamation marks, question marks, speech marks, apostrophes

question mark a punctuation mark that is used to show that a question has been asked

report a piece of non-fiction writing that describes a place, event, etc.

rhyme when words rhyme, they share a sound – face/space/race/plaice all rhyme

shape poem a poem written in a shape that is relevant to the poem

simile using a simile is a way of describing something by saying it is like something else. 'The cat sounded like a motorbike as it purred and rumbled' is a simile

singular describes one thing. 'Cat' is the singular, and 'cats' is the plural

skimming reading quickly to get an understanding of a piece of writing

speech marks used on either side of a sentence or phrase when you want to show that someone is speaking

stick (on a letter) part of some letters, e.g. d, b, etc.

story a piece of fictional writing

syllables chunks of sound in a word. The word 'caterpillar' has four syllables: cat–er–pill–ar

tail (on a letter) part of some letters, e.g. y, g, etc.

tense the tense of a verb tells you when something happened

tongue-twister where a letter or sound is repeated and a sentence is hard to say such as 'Peter painted pretty plant pots'

upper case letters another way of saying 'capitals'. ABCDE letters... are upper case letters

verb doing words – running, climbing, saying, etc. All actions are verbs

vocabulary words